Anthony's Prayers

Thank You Father for Everlasting

Anthony's Prayers: Thank You Father for Everlasting copyright 2011 by Anthony Torrone.

All rights reserved. Published 2011. Printed at Color House Graphics, Grand Rapids, Michigan in the United States of America.

No part of this book may be reproduced, stored or transmitted in any form or by any means without written permission. For information address Freeze Frame Publishing, 10383 36th Street, Lowell MI 49331.

Photography copyright 2011 by Lance Wynn.

Cover by Lance Wynn

Photos on pages 14, 15, 16, 17 courtesy of The Grand Rapids Press.
Photos on pages 12, 13, 17 courtesy of the Ter Maat family.
Photos on pages 21, 40 courtesy of the DeVree family.
Photo on pages 8, 9 courtesy of Servant's Community Church.

For information about special discounts for bulk purchases, please contact:
Freeze Frame Publishing Special Sales at AnthonysPrayers@FreezeFramePublishing.com.

Grateful acknowledgement is made to The Grand Rapids Press for permission to reprint previously published material. And to Sarah VanDyken for transcribing Anthony's original manuscript; to the DeVree family; to the Ter Maat family; to Servant's Community Church; to the businesses in Anthony's neighborhood; and to the many friends of Anthony without whom his prayer book, his dream, would not be possible.

If you would like more information on Anthony and his West Side neighborhood, please visit AnthonysPrayers.blogspot.com

Library of Congress Control Number: 2011942059

Torrone, Anthony 1955-

ISBN 978-0-9839868-0-5

Anthony's Prayers
Thank You Father for Everlasting

by
Anthony Torrone

Edited by
Charles Honey
Pat Shellenbarger

Photography and Design
Lance Wynn

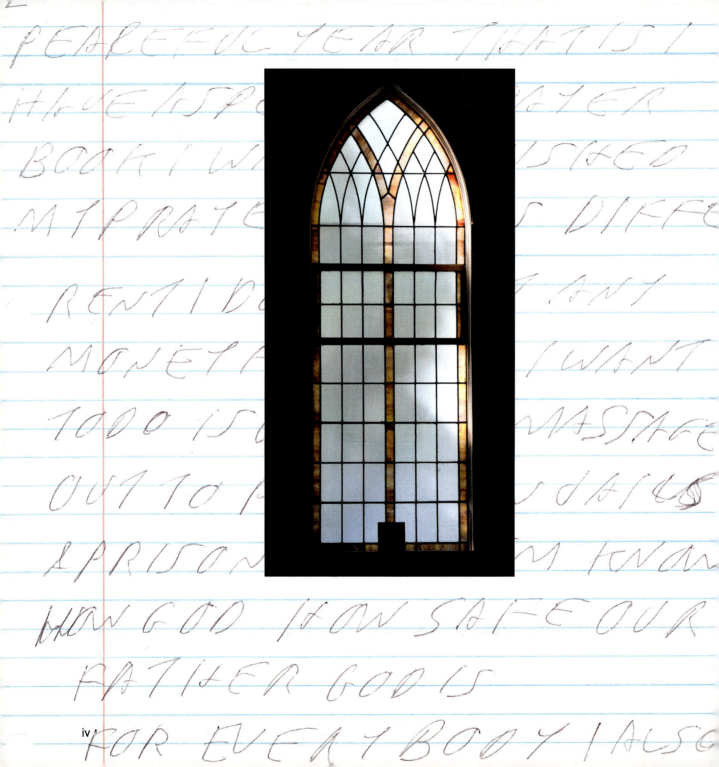

Foreword

This is Anthony Torrone's prayer book. That might seem obvious from the author's name on the cover, but to understand the significance of Anthony writing a prayer book, you must know more about him. Although he never attended school--at least not in the sense most of us think of school--and while no one ever taught him to read or write, Anthony sat down one day and began writing about all those things for which he was thankful. He doesn't bother with punctuation, and spelling isn't his strong suit. His words of praise pour out in a stream of consciousness.

> *"I thank you father that I was born in united states of America and I thank you very much that I can live in united states where I can trust you love you keep you into my heart 7 days a week and I also thank you father that I can live normal in America."*

A lesser person might find many reasons to be anything but thankful. Anthony is developmentally disabled, apparently a result of a flulike illness when he was two years old. But he also has characteristics of a savant, including an artistic knack for building elaborate creations from Lego blocks. He has thousands of Legos in his apartment, most sorted into plastic tubs and others embedded in his sculptures, such as a miniature Statue of Liberty, a model of the house where his mother raised him, a riverboat the size of a coffee table, and stacks upon stacks of signs he sees on his walks and recreates from memory.

He has an uncanny memory for detail. He never forgets a birthday. Tell him your date of birth, and Anthony can tell you how many days you've been alive. Tell him the date and time of your birth, and he can tell you how many hours you've been on Earth. He can't explain how he does it.

"It's a gift from God," he said. That's his standard answer for many good things in his life.

He is 56 years old, eternally cheerful, unfailingly optimistic and seldom dwells on the less glorious times of his life. When he was nine years old, Anthony's mother reluctantly placed him in the Willowbrook State School on Staten Island, NY, unaware of the deplorable conditions. He was abused physically and emotionally.

When he was praying one day, "a nurse told me to shut my mouth didn't like my prayers," he wrote nearly five decades later.

"I was tied up with a rope once I couldn't move my stomach back & forth A nurse hit me in my mouth too with a baseball bat knocked my front tooth out... I also was afraid the world was coming to an end...

"When all of these things was going on all the time I was afraid it wont end wont stop will continue for the rest of my life I was scared it wont get any better for the rest of my life... I couldnt do nothing about it All I did was be patient seven days a week until I left that tragedy place Mon January sixteenth nineteen sixty seven 12 pm...

"My Lord Savior God helped me survive..."

After Anthony's mother, Nellie Torrone, removed him from Willowbrook in 1967, investigations exposed the appalling treatment of children there. The State of New York closed Willowbrook in 1987.

Anthony doesn't dwell on those years-- "one thousand twenty seven days of my life," he wrote--preferring to focus on how much better his life is now. His mother moved with him to a small home on Grand Rapids' West Side in 1971, or, to be more precise, "Monday, Oct. 18, 1971, at 4 o'clock. There wasn't even a cloud in the sky," he said.

There she raised him and shielded him from the negative influence of the outside world, such as children who called him names and adults who might take advantage of a young man's childlike innocence. In his new neighborhood, Anthony made friends easily and never forgot a kindness. Four decades ago, when Ed DeVree saw 16-year-old Anthony sitting alone in church, he offered him a mint and cemented their friendship for life. Ed died some years ago, but his widow, Belva, still includes Anthony in her family's gatherings.

Others in the neighborhood were similarly drawn to the young man with his gentle, innocent manner and his abiding faith in God and the goodness of mankind. "He's just a loving, gentle man," Rev. Richard Ter Maat said. "We're all blessed to know him."

Anthony took a job sweeping floors and stocking shelves at the Fulton Pharmacy a few blocks from his home. When he learned recently the pharmacy soon would close, he wrote a special prayer:

"I also thank you father for all kinds of friends at the pharmacy store with lots of odd jobs & with lots of love"

He still shovels snow, helps his elderly neighbors and picks up cans and bottles for money.

In 1998, Anthony heard his mother scream and found her at the bottom of their basement stairway. Nellie Torrone died of her injuries the following day, leaving Anthony's future uncertain. She left her meager estate to a niece in Pennsylvania with the understanding she would take care of Anthony. Instead, the niece sold the house and furnishings, kept the money, and put Anthony in an adult foster home across town from the neighborhood he had come to love.

Anthony was miserable, and the people in his old neighborhood missed his cheery presence, so they moved him back to an apartment just down the street from the home where his mother had raised him. He resumed his place in the West Side social structure, living independently, greeting neighbors, helping out where he can and writing every day in his journal.

For those lucky enough to know him, Anthony is as much a West Side fixture as Frank's Market, the butcher shop where he hangs out each morning chatting with employees. Carrying his customary bag of bottles, he greets passers-by with a broad grin and a cheerful quip, then pops into The Bitter End coffeehouse and shares his latest hopes and dreams with the regulars.

For some, a chance meeting with Anthony brightens their day. This book may do the same for you.

Anthony hopes his prayer book inspires others to find God and forego sin--in his words, to "make people understand God is a safe father." It's also his way of thanking God for all he has, not so much the material possessions--for by most standards, he doesn't have much--but for the less tangible things many of us take for granted: the freedom to live our lives in dignity with friends who love and accept us as we are.

Charles Honey   Grand Rapids, Michigan
Pat Shellenbarger   November, 2011
Friends of Anthony

YOU DONT HACE TO PAY M
FOR MY PRAYER BOOK PUBLI
IT IS A U WANT I WANT TO D
GOD A FAVOR CAUSE GOD HAS
BEEN DOING ME LOTS OF GOOD
FAVORS FOR LOTS OF YEARS &
DOING GOD A FAVOR IS TO
THANK HIM I LOVE GOD ALSO
I WANT MY PRAYER BOOK TO
BE A FREE & A GIFT TO YOU &
EVERYBODY DONT PAY ME
FOR MY BOOK LET IT BE FRE
FOR YOU & PEOPLE IN THE

I thought this book would get more people to love you
to trust you
and to believe you
to help tell people if they ask you to come in there heart
and to keep you in there
that there life will be good and normal
this book father is to help people understand your rules from the bible

~ Anthony

I naby down the sleep
and I pray the Lord my so the keep
if I should die before I wake
my so the take

I'm glad my mom had brought me up good
and right
and took good care of me
and that is why living by myself has
helped me a lot
I want to continue father to life by myself
in your way

dear heavenly Father
I want to thank you for giving me a right mom in staten island in 1955
I want to thank you for helping me be born the healthy way
thank you for all the good babys food my mom has fed me
also all the good care and all the good fun I had
as I was getting older and big enough

thank you for bacon eggs toast juice coffee my mom has made me
thank you so much Father for all the clothes shoes soxs
my mom has been buying me every year
thank you for helping my mom take good care of me
and doing her best for me
you did a good job Father

Original members of Servant's Community Church. Anthony, 26, is third from the right.

I thank you that my mom did not get rid of me
or give me up
and I want to thank you father for letting her take good care of me
and for keeping my life good and happy and healthy and normal
and as I was growing up healthy
and normal
and happy
and gifted

thank you Father for allowing my mom to love me every day
7 days each week 365 days a year
also 366 days every four years
without troubles
and without problems
also without arguments

I want to thank you for letting me live right
live normal
live healthy without convulsions
also without seizures
and I havnt had any of it happen to me since sun oct 27 74 1030 pm

Thank you for letting me do my own shopping
and I went to thank you for helping me take my medicine on my own
without being told
I want to thank you for letting me live by myself
in my own quiet apartment

I want to thank you for helping me learn to ride buses by myself
I want to thank you for helping me go to kmart
toys r us Meijer target and walmart
to buy special Legos for my own ideas

thank you father for a good special Lego set
I got on Christmas from the Lego co
for all kinds of Lego space sets and things for the city
and for helping me learn all kinds of art designs
on my own with out any help

thank you for the new colors of Legos they come out with
for bunch of pink bricks
also purple bricks
light green light blue and white
thank you for helping me make real normal designs
for helping me add more new real signs to my art designs
for helping my mom believe me and understand me

I want to thank you for helping me do things
on my own for my mom when she was around
I want to thank you for helping me cut her grass on my own
and go grocery shopping

I want to thank you for a special kind of mom
I enjoyed my mother a lot
it was a very good special presentation
and kind and thoughtful too

I want to thank you very much Father
for helping my mom every year
on thanksgiving and Christmas
for special dinners
also key lime pies she made me

I want to thank you for helping me doing a good job
and doing that is my favorite hobby
and I enjoy doing it in your way
and I appreciated it
sorry my mom is not here to see it

I also want to thank you
for helping make my self a very special art work design
that is a cemetery grave stone of my moms
im happy I still have it

I also want to thank mom for bringing me
to Grand Rapids Mon Oct 1971 at 4pm
without a cloud in to the sky
and I want to thank you very much Father
for very special friends at ninth reformed church
with lots of love
lots of joy
lots of understanding
lots of thoughts

I like living down the street from my moms old house
when I look at it helps me think of her
remember her
thanks for the memories

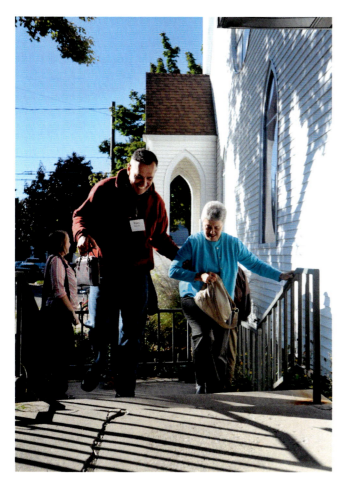

I want my life to be a little bit more better
and a little bit more easyer
a little bit more safer
also little bit more happy
little bit more peaceful
with lots of love and lots of smiles
and with lots of kind less
safe and sound in your way

I want to thank you father that I have a good porch
to sit on in the summer months
I want to thank you that I can have my meals on my porch
and my coffee on the porch in the summer months
and I thank you that nobody is here to stop me

I want to thank you for letting me be on my own.
I thank you father that I don't half to live into any special homes
with to many people
I thank you for the private quiet apartment

living alone helps keep my life happy
and also normal
and father as longes I'm able to live by myself
and on my own
I want to continue to trust you
believe you

living by myself and on my own
helps prevent me from hearing bad words
and living by myself without hearing bad words
is what helps me be a Christian
and to trust you and believe you
and it helps make my life normal

I promise you I wont leave my northwest side again
I promise you I won't live in to no more group homes again
I also promise you father I won't let nothing make me cry
I promise nobody is not make fun of me again
like they did in my early life

I dont want to be teased again
all I want to do is live like a good growing up man
I also want to thank you that nobody hasnt picked on me
in a long time

I thank you father that my friends never let me down
I thank you father that I have them close to me when I need them
I thank you father for helping my friends keep me in to grand rapids close to them

I want to say thank you for helping Ed and Bel pick me so fast
as a yard worker and snow shoveler
I want to thank you for letting Belva and Ed taking me out to eat
in restaurants on my birthday
and on Christmas every year
also thank you for the special Lego sets they been buying me
it has helped me learn normal things

thank you father for my special friend Dick Helen termaat
thank you for money and gift certificates
they giving me on my birthday and Christmas
and for protecting me from things I don't like
thank you very much Father for letting me be part of the familys
to the termaat and also to the Devrees

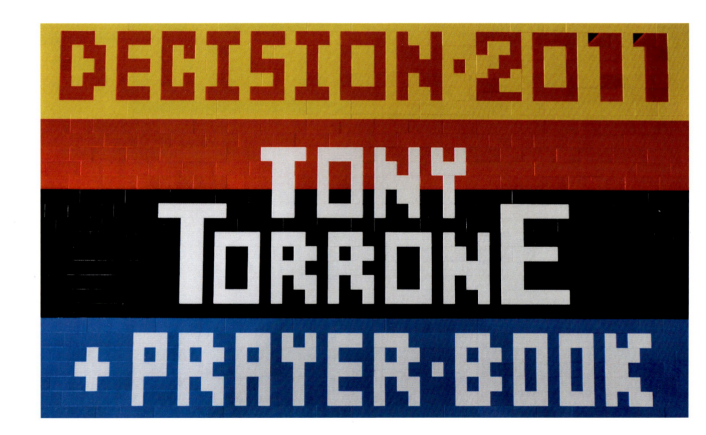

thank you for helping me make my own decision
writing my own book
without being told
without school
without college
without home work
also without any school teachers

I also like this book to be the best seller
help bring lesson people that there is a god
I want everybody to read it on a rainy day
or rainy night

that is what my special good religious book I'm writing is all about father
is also to thank you for all the good normal things you did for me
you are my special #1 lord savior in heaven

I thank you father that I don't have any sufferings
and I thank you for not letting me sit on a hard concrete cold institution floor

if it wasn't for you father I just don't know what I do
you living into my heart helps make life easy
and normal for me 7 days a week
and it is just like having a home and a roof over your head
I love you and believe you father

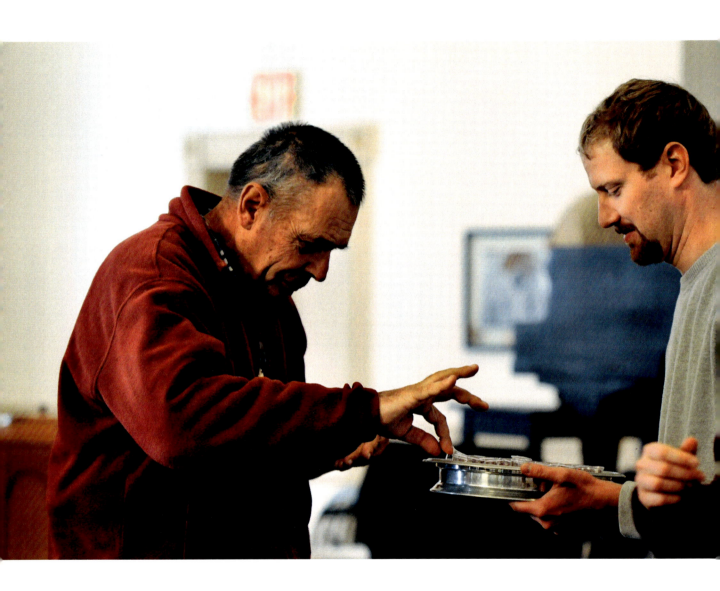

when it is time for me to die
Im going to be up into heaven this way
and when I go up into heaven
I will see you face to face
I'm also going to have a good time
I won't half to worrie about what is going on earth
or hear bad things again
heaven will be a new home with freedom

thank you father
I say all of this to you in Jesus name we pray
amen amen

About the Author

Anthony Torrone, 56, is a longtime citizen of Grand Rapids, Michigan, and a beloved resident of the city's West Side. He is a member of Servant's Community Church, formerly known as Ninth Reformed Church, which he began attending at the age of 16. He writes daily in his journal. This is his first published book.